HUNGER
IN THE
DESERT
Love Poems

REBECCA MITCHELL-GUTHRIE

Hunger in the Desert: Love Poems
Published by Poet Press Publishing
Scottsdale, AZ

ISBN: 979-8-218-06895-0
POETRY / Subjects & Themes / Love

For lovers of love.

CONTENTS

Pottery	6
Ironwood Tree Nectar	8
White Tiger	10
Mesquite Seed Pod	12
I Know You Just Enough	14
Piñata	16
Fire	18
Desert Spiritual Homeland	20
Lure	22
Prickly Pear Cactus Fruit	24
Southwest Moon	26
Zoo	28
Waiting	30
Gourd	32
Southern Hug	34
Blue Flame	36
Shore	38
Starlings	40
Egg	42
Sunlight on the Water	44
Wishing Well	46
Nap Heaven	48
Stone	50
Maze	52
Dark Chocolate	54
The Longing	56
Emerald	58
Watershed	60
Valentine	62
Drum	64
Cataract	66
Rosary	68
Veil	70
For a Million Years	72
Beside Me	74
Love or Grief	76
Pink Sunset	78

POTTERY

Found, unearthed.

Broken pieces.

Perfect together.

Ironwood Tree Nectar

I imagine moving my fingers down your back,

your skin, silky, like little downy globes

on creosote, your body, in sharp contrast

to the serrated spines in this desert landscape,

spikes of ocotillo, splashed in scarlet, or massive,

thorny saguaro, crowned with white blooms.

Bees, crazy in love with ironwood buds, awash

in lavender, hum like the cueing of an orchestra.

Obsessed with this nectar, nothing else matters.

WHITE TIGER

The sound of your voice unlocks

a thousand cages within me.

This white tiger, weak and wild, hungers.

Mesquite
Seed Pod

Because the eyes love without argument,

they can embrace your human body

when my mouth cannot tell you

and my arms cannot reach for you.

Next time I see you, I will look at your face

and linger, take you in like a seed in the desert,

saturated, swollen, about to open,

because *finally, there is rain.*

I Know You Just Enough

I know you just enough to know it might bother me

to know much more about your sweetness,

how your body would feel in my hands,

that you'd wrestle my problems as your own.

See, I don't think you can be mine,

but you'd have me forever if I knew you

just a little bit more.

Piñata

I was blindfolded.

I believed that our little party together

would be glorious if you opened

like a piñata, colorful candy

spilling from your brilliant mind,

confetti flying around,

trinkets and sweet things.

The stick inside my head,

I waved it around and missed,

too hard toward you.

So, you swung away from me.

Instead, now, I *love* my way to you.

In my horrible dark night of the soul

I must wish *only* for your happiness,

even if it does not include me.

FIRE

To grow this fire, add kindling.

Strike your one match with surgical precision.

Breathe it into being and back away for a moment.

Stoke, tame it.

Watch with careful attention, adjust things gently

until it glows bright, hot.

Desert Spiritual Homeland

I've always wanted to fall in love and run away

to this desert, scorched by day, cool at night.

I marry you, commit to your landscape,

faithful despite scorpions and Gila monsters,

for better, for worse.

Here, red rock dust settles in my heart,

between saguaros and dry wash basins,

where magnolias and kudzu of my past

no longer complicate my view.

Startled by the Sun, dangerous and blinding,

there's nowhere to hide.

LURE

I had cast myself so far out into your whitewater

that I couldn't reel myself back in.

My lure, embellished with feathers and ribbons,

sharp and dangerous,

was ripped away by cold, rushing water

and lost in the current,

cutting river grass as it went.

Prickly Pear Cactus Fruit

Mysterious and ripe, you would be soft,

scarlet red on my tongue.

I want to hold you, but I am afraid.

Getting past all those spikes

and thorns could make me bleed.

SOUTHWEST MOON

I hike at sunrise, missing you.

You seem so far away,

waning and translucent in the western sky,

floating above the shoulder of the desert ridge.

Months ago, I dreamed that my father gave me

a pendant of the Moon to match my pendant

of the Sun.

When I woke, I asked, why the Moon?

Now, I understand.

One is the Sun, visible, daily, sustaining,

and you, Moon, are quiet and hidden.

Both hold me, Earth, in delicate balance.

I orbit her, you orbit me.

One is light, and the other, a tidal pull.

Zoo

When you left me, the doors, crates, and coops

in my zoo became unhinged.

Things escaped, flew, galloped,

slithered, crawled, waddled, or swung out

on big hairy arms, rubbery feet,

or wings into my lost city,

leaving a big mess.

So in love with you,

now I just blink at my screen,

feathers float down around me.

Waiting

God sprinkles angel dust between us.

It drifts around the room,

falling like snow in my hot hands.

I linger in this blizzard

like the Hanged Man in the Tarot,

waiting in tattered cards, suspended,

watching from upside down.

Blood runs to my head.

Maybe I will freeze to death

or pass out with my halo intact,

unable to move and longing for you.

GOURD

A gourd grows in the meadow,

hidden beneath the grasses,

and wrapped in soft straw

from last year's plumes.

Quietly, it keeps faith

in being found and scooped hollow

as a cup to nourish.

A river bends nearby,

and even the summer rains

do not overflow to threaten

the destiny of the gourd

and the lovers who will drink from it.

SOUTHERN HUG

My Southern hug feels hot and sticky,

tastes like sweet, iced tea,

sounds like cicadas,

enchants like magnolia,

and leaves a little Spanish moss in your hair.

BLUE FLAME

My love burns, scorches what it touches.

I hide this blue flame away

for your protection, inside me.

Ashes fall on my feet.

SHORE

I waited too patiently for you to dive off

that little boat and swim to shore.

I stood on the beach,

my feet in burning hot sand,

a red flower in my hair.

Finally, I turned and walked away,

waves erasing my hope.

STARLINGS

This sweet connection is murmuration,

sacred union, fated by design.

Flight path natural, instinctive, magical,

attuned in perfect measure.

The dance of a thousand fragile wings,

oh, *my anguish*, as they fly away.

EGG

Your semipermeable membrane skin,

made of calcium crystals,

is just tough enough to hold a soft, yellow sun.

Runs when opened, must be held carefully.

Sunlight on
the Water

Love, like sunlight on the water,

does not decide where it falls

but instead, allows.

It does not break the light

but bends, stretches, and reshapes it,

like luminescent fireflies

who play inside the swell.

Like this light, you move within my soul,

refracting through my skin and bone,

in blind advance to the depth

until your horizontal glow

spreads throughout the blue.

WISHING WELL

This tenderness is a wishing well,

like words I drop into you.

I wonder, what is their worth,

waiting to be gathered, valued, spent.

Ripples move me in circles,

rhythms of energy,

pushing out against the edges,

falling, I glimmer in the sunlight.

Nap Heaven

We don't have to die to get there.

Wrapping my arm across your hips,

I let my fingertips follow the curve of your shirt.

I listen to your rise and fall.

I roll in close to hear the thump,

the heartbeat on your neck.

My lips are near your ear.

I whisper, *I love you.*

STONE

There is so much I need to tell you,

but I could only do it if I lie down next to you

in this river where leaves gather at your shoulders.

I would lay my head on your naked chest,

ear against your breast, my tears on your warm skin,

like water on a stone, shaping you slowly.

Maze

I am in a maze of towering hedges of evergreen,

trying to find a way to give my affection,

but my hands are bound. Trees block exploration

from giving you my heart, from knowing your life,

from touching you with my words and laughter.

I am lost in this labyrinth,

a soul who wishes to love completely.

Dark Chocolate

It's complicated.

I like your edges, semi-sweet,

matter-of-fact style,

and unassuming, bitter bite.

Wrapped in gold paper,

you are intense chocolate, 88%.

Unexpectedly badass, but is it good for me?

THE LONGING

I developed a relationship

with my longing for you.

And now I miss the longing.

It kept me company in my car,

in my bed, in my head.

Now, I do not know who I am

without it, without you.

So, do I cry for you or the longing?

I do not know.

EMERALD

Heartbreak advances through my body like war,

leaving fields of burnt corn,

wide-eyed corpses, and smoke,

because I can see you are holding a gemstone,

my glowing, emerald heart.

I stare in amazement at this scene unfolding,

watching you turn it over, touching it.

I want to say don't love it so much,

but it is too late.

You love looking at your secret treasure,

rarer than a diamond.

Its worn, beveled edges grow warm

from the heat of your hands.

Nobody knows that you have it.

WATERSHED

It starts small, a drip from my heart,

from my breasts and hips.

First in little trickles, mountain streams flow

to thunderous rivers that push ice,

trees, mud, and rock, flooding to the ocean,

into you.

VALENTINE

The rose petals are brittle,

dropping on the dining room table.

The chocolate was eaten,

the card is now a bookmark,

but the love remains.

DRUM

This indigo night in the canyon

where the hawk hunts,

the stars and I gather

under the Moon to worship you.

In my hands, you come alive,

pulsing and breathing,

like coyotes moving swiftly

between the rocks.

With you set between my thighs,

I feel your drumbeat everywhere.

Cataract

I am filled with emotion today.

Moon's face is full and peering down

into a tiny eye on Earth.

What I look at is not simply a pond in the woods

whose trees have gathered around in the autumn

to shed their leaves, leaving a film upon its surface

like a cataract, milky and obscured.

It is something more, an awareness.

One day I will grieve for the time

when your own eye was clear, vibrant, and young.

ROSARY

Silken and spun like a spider web,

you have been nearly ripped apart

by abuse and violence,

a hand across your backside, or by the wind.

But your holy strand is a thread unbroken

that floats, exposed and cool enough

for love to condense on its surface,

to repair and renew like a rosary

sparkling with beaded dew.

VEIL

When you die, in an instant I am here,

and you are there.

And though this veil between us is thin,

like onionskin paper,

I can only see you from this other side.

You'll be so young again.

I close my eyes, pull you close,

feel your warmth, wishing,

just one more time with you,

because in this moment you are here,

alive and safe in my arms.

For a Million Years

When you die before me and leave me here

without your heart to see me through,

I will yearn for a million years,

forever, for everything, for you.

BESIDE ME

Beside me no one lies, yet I swear

I can hear you breathing still.

Through the window I see

branches etched in a lavender sky,

a silver Moon washing over it

like a watercolor painting,

layers of transparency

revealing my heartache.

I wonder what my life would be like

if you were beside me now?

LOVE OR GRIEF

Separated at birth are two lakes

divided only by reeds.

Water bleeds into one,

all mixed up inside your heart.

Overlapping like panes of antique glass,

undulating and distorted,

you cannot tell them apart.

PINK SUNSET

Our footprints on the beach

will wash away with the next wave,

and if not that one, then the next,

or maybe the wave after that.

And your memory that we walked together

may wash away with the next breath,

and if not that one, then the next.

The sand, pink sunset, sea oats, shells in your hand,

and breaking waves might not remember.

I will.

*Thank you to Kitty Collier Mingus, my chosen sister,
for friendship since childhood; to Teri Bloom and
Joseph Hummel for patient encouragement. Thank
you to Jennifer Jas for editorial guidance, Polly
Letofsky for her expertise and spunk, and Victoria
Wolf for her technical skills and vision.*

*Special thanks to Carol Fountain Nix for her
exquisite hand-inked calligraphy subtitle, for our
enduring friendship and creative partnership. Thank
you to my mother-in-law, Pickett Guthrie,
for believing in me.*

*I give my deepest appreciation to Polly
Mitchell-Guthrie for love and support in
my creative writing and life journey*

Rebecca Mitchell-Guthrie is a clairvoyant medium,

life coach, artist, teacher, and author. She lives in

Arizona, adoring the Sun, Moon, and the stars.

www.ingramcontent.com/pod-product-compliance
Lightning Source LLC
Chambersburg PA
CBHW021336160726
47994CB00007B/2725